High-Performance
Learning
Communities

The Practicing Administrator's Leadership Series
Jerry J. Herman and Janice L. Herman, Editors

ROADMAPS
TO SUCCESS

Other Titles in This Series Include:

(see back cover for additional titles)

High-Performance Learning Communities

Dian K. Castle
Nolan Estes

CORWIN PRESS, INC.
A Sage Publications Company
Thousand Oaks, California

For information address:

Corwin Press, Inc.
A Sage Publications Company
2455 Teller Road
Thousand Oaks, California 91320

SAGE Publications Ltd.
6 Bonhill Street
London EC2A 4PU
United Kingdom

SAGE Publications India Pvt. Ltd.
M-32 Market
Greater Kailash I
New Delhi 110 048 India

Printed in the United States of America

Library of Congress Cataloging-in-Publication Data

Castle, Dian K.
　　High-performance learning communities / Dian K. Castle, Nolan Estes.
　　　　p.　cm. — (Roadmaps to success)
　　Includes bibliographical references (p. 60-68)
　　ISBN 0-8039-6180-4
　　1. School management and organization—United States.
　2. Educational change—United States.　3. Education—Social aspects—United States.　I. Estes, Nolan.　II. Title.　III. Series.
　LB2805.C35　1994
　371.2′00973—dc20　　　　　　　　　　　　　　　　　　　94-23861

This book is printed on acid-free paper.

95　96　97　98　99　10　9　8　7　6　5　4　3　2　1

Corwin Press Production Editor: Marie Louise Penchoen

Contents

Foreword

High-Performance Learning Communities, written by Dian Castle and Nolan Estes, presents an impassioned plea for dramatic changes to be made in the way school districts are organized and in their current operational methods. In addition, they ask that schools develop operational relationships with all other societal elements. They suggest that dramatic changes are required in the content, processes, and structure of school districts in the United States if they are to produce students who will be able to successfully compete in the multinational world environment of the future.

Although we believe that a few readers may take issue with some of the statements and concepts presented in this book, the model created by the authors is a thinking person's challenge for all who are concerned with the education of our children and youth. Included is a special appeal for those who want excellent results to become change agents themselves in order to lead their communities toward a major paradigm shift that represents a systemically changed and greatly improved educational system.

The authors provide numerous examples and graphic illustrations to clarify and emphasize the various elements of their model. They also identify a variety of leadership districts that are already implementing some of the principles discussed in the book. You will find a convenient checklist to guide the systematic planning of high-performance learning activities. Finally, annotated references will assist those who wish to learn more about leadership and change in High-Performance Learning Communities.

JERRY J. HERMAN
JANICE L. HERMAN
Series Co-Editors

About the Authors

Dian K. Castle, Ed.D., is President and Founder of Educational Consultants 1, a firm that serves school systems and their leaders who vision educational renewal. She is a past Director of Staff Development for the Kansas State Department of Education and a past Director of Human Resource Development for the Texas State Department of Mental Health and Mental Retardation. Her previous experience includes positions in elementary and secondary teaching, counseling, and administration; Human Resource Development adjunct faculty member; Manager for Professional Course and Curriculum Development for BellSouth Services; Director of soft-money projects, including a Title XX educational/vocational project for AFDC recipients; social worker for the Will County Department of Public Aid, Joliet, IL; and recreation leader for the City of Philadelphia Department of Recreation.

Dian Castle has published numerous articles in education and training, including key research used in the Exemplary Performer. Castle also presents annually at national education and training conferences. She has designed the curriculum for both the Cooperative Superintendency Program at the University of Texas at Austin and the Professional Leadership Academy of the Urban Education Laboratory for the Kansas City, Missouri, School District. Currently, she is a consultant for the management development program for Head Start Directors and executive staff.

Nolan Estes (Harvard University, Ph.D.) is L.D. Haskew Centennial Professor of Public School Administration and Director of the Cooperative Superintendency Program in Austin, Texas. He has been the recipient of various honors and awards, including Texas Educator of the Year from *Texas Business Magazine* and National Educator of the Year from the National Coalition of Title I Parents.

Estes is Director of the nationally recognized Executive Leadership Program at The University of Texas at Austin.

He has been a principal, assistant superintendent, and superintendent in both suburban and urban school districts. As a Ford Fellow Intern, Estes went to the Office of Education in Washington, D.C., and was later named Associate Commissioner for Elementary and Secondary Education, taking responsibility for the National TTT Program (Trainers of Trainers of Teachers).

Estes has been an educational television instructor with Baylor University and the Texas Education Agency, a member of the Center for Field Studies at Harvard Graduate School of Education, a visiting professor at the University of Chattanooga and the University of Arizona, and a professorial assistant at Harvard University. He is the author of numerous publications and is sought as a speaker by education groups nationwide.

Introduction

Economic and social forces are causing many organizations, including educational institutions, to rethink the way they do business. American schools served the industrial age better than any other system, but they fail to adequately support today's knowledge-based economy. As Alvin Toffler stated in his book, *Power Shift*, the new economy forces us

> to rethink all . . . ideas developed during the smokestack era. The very categories are now obsolete. . . . No nation can operate a 21st century economy without a 21st century electronic infrastructure embracing computers, data communications, and the other new media. This requires a population as familiar with this informational infrastructure as it is with cars, roads, highways, trains, and the transportation infrastructure of the smokestack period (1991, pp. 368-69).

Competitive pressures are demanding that American public school systems answer immediately with improved quality, service, and responsiveness. Even the most successful and promising of school systems must develop new techniques if it is to survive as more than a mere custodian of our youth. The opportunity is now! To reinvent their school systems, educational managers may need to

abandon the organizational and operational principles and procedures they are now using and create entirely new ones. These new
techniques focus on the efficiency and effectiveness of core education processes. Progressive educational managers will integrate operational, technical, and educational knowledge to optimize
performance in terms of cost, service, time, and quality. Educational
research calls this process restructuring and business calls it re-
engineering. The authors call it by its result—a high-performance
learning community.

The concept of high-performance learning communities grows
out of a sizable body of recent research about what does and does not
work in educating children. Some of these findings are included in
the annotated bibliography that accompanies this book. The research takes into account the needs of both families and communities. In addition, several change management and organization
development strategies are involved. The uniqueness of the high-
performance learning community is that it brings together techniques that produce an integrated and systematic delivery system
during several stages of education—birth, transition, and renewal.
This approach of actively designing America's future combines
planning, instruction, curriculum, materials usage, staff development, community/business linkages, funding, and accountability
into a flexible and comprehensive system.

High-performance learning communities represent the product
of complex transformational cultural change and are a radical approach to improving education. They do not fix anything; they begin
from scratch! Herein lies the notion of identifying and abandoning
the outdated rules and fundamental assumptions of a bygone era
that underlie current educational operations. School systems cannot be high-performance learning communities with only superfi-
cial reorganizations that are no more effective than rearranging the
furniture. School-based decision making or site-based management is an example of such a failure. Overlaying a new organization on top of an old process is like pouring soured wine into an
attractive decanter.

A well-functioning Total Quality Management program improves
an organization incrementally over time, in contrast to the immediate
and total rule-changing nature of a high-performance learning com-

munity. Typically, a TQM program is ongoing and is used to maintain and continuously enhance products and services. It tends to fix things by making marginal improvements to current processes. Numerous school reforms of the past 2 decades fall into this category. Nevertheless, a successful high-performance learning community will find TQM invaluable in retaining every advantage achieved through dramatic changes to the core education processes.

This book dedicates itself to the exploration of high-performance learning communities, addressing the following areas:

- The need for systemic and systematic change in the reinvention of the American school system
- The attributes that characterize high-performance learning communities
- The knowledge base, acts of leadership, and performance skills that prepare educational leaders to create, lead, and manage high-performance learning communities
- Resources for educational leaders to use to establish high-performance learning communities

We have included a variety of examples of educational communities that are making significant progress toward the model we describe, although no one system has yet to demonstrate all attributes of the high-performance learning community. We commend the efforts of all those who are choosing not to remain passive or apathetic, and who are doing what is right in the best interests of children.

Awakening to the Need for Systemic and Systematic Change

Rationale

Economic, social, cultural, demographic, political, and technological realities require a new system of education not only to compete but to survive. The information age in which we live demands that America create an educational system that provides the necessary technical knowledge and competence to thrive in the international marketplace. Today's global economy is based on high skills, and high skills are prerequisite to high wages. At the same time, escalating divorce rates and increasing numbers of children born to single mothers, coupled with the climbing rate of immigration, increase the risk of childhood poverty. Associated with poverty are serious health and living problems, such as increased infant mortality, childhood illness, teenage pregnancy, youth homicide and suicide, and drug and alcohol abuse. One third of America's preschool children are destined for school failure because of poverty, neglect, illness, handicapping conditions, and a lack of parental protection and nurturance (*Statistical Abstract*, 1989).

America faces a moment of history as it embarks upon a course to rid itself of the virtual anarchy that the school system appears to represent. It is a moment of unprecedented breakthrough as we design a different school, a school that can meet the demands of the 21st century. This is the potential of the high-performance learning community.

The creation of this new school is basically a local initiative where everyone is responsible. Parents cannot send their children to school and then absolve themselves of any further responsibility. Educators cannot blame their failures on the family, society, board of education, or taxpayer. CEOs cannot herald the school system for its productive values and then criticize the same system when it has a poor yield. The well-being of America's children depends upon more than partnerships between business, industry, and schools. All sectors must *collaborate* in the change plan and the strategies process. The James Comer (1990) and Luvern Cunningham (1990) research, for example, deals with education as a community responsibility. The community must focus all of its services—health, family, human services, business, and so on—upon learners in accordance with their individual needs in order to ensure their academic success and full employment.

What Is It?

Systemic and systematic change is required to reinvent the education system. This reconstitution encompasses more than reform initiatives. It necessitates more than the incremental adjustment of policy, regulation, and structure; it calls for much more than the tweaking of educational processes, practices, and procedures that have characterized the rhetoric of reform. During the last 20 years, have seen billions of dollars poured into education with little or no return on our investment. Reforms have merely spelled higher drop-out rates, lower achievement scores, and decreased attendance in institutions of higher education.

Systemic change is defined by two overriding focal aspects. The first of these involves the primary components of the system—

their design and interrelationships. These components represent the core education processes and include a) curriculum—standards, delivery, and assessment; teacher recruitment, selection, development, evaluation, and compensation; b) teaching—methods and media; c) community involvement—business, industry, government, the professions, and taxpayer; student support systems; and d) governance—role, products, and services. The second aspect of systemic reform is concerned with planning, implementing, managing, sustaining, and evaluating complex change.

On the other hand, systematic change is a game plan or methodology, a procedural model for performing systemic change. To achieve systemic change there must be a systematic approach. The checklist and sample lesson plan presented later in the book contain information relevant to systematic change and the creation of high-performance learning communities. These materials constitute an integrated methodology that is meant to challenge the core education processes. This is a "living" methodology and subject to the constant iteration of ideas and lessons brought about by the very execution of the methodology. It is action research. Following this structured yet flexible tack, American public schools may achieve an environment in which performance continuously improves and where action is taken to ensure that the improvements are sustainable through building a cultural environment that fosters and embraces change.

Result

High-performance learning communities built on the foundation of systemic and systematic change are able to deliver quality goods and services to customers which ultimately affects the health of the whole system. They collectively do much more than set goals, solve problems at hand, or even manage performance. Instead, they respond to a climate of rapid change with holistic leadership that not only identifies potentials but also strategically manages the course of metasystem delivery and evaluation.

High-performance learning communities reflect the compelling and central interest of the child as learner. The performance of learners is the critical criterion for the continued existence of the educational entity—whatever structure it assumes as a result of local design. The following characteristics reflect a high-performing learning community, the best educational system if we are ever truly to serve children:

- *A shared vision* of a strategically-managed and nurturing, outcome-based learning environment in which high standards of health, education, and social development are achieved by all learners. There is the active participation of parents, business, health care providers, social service organizations, civic organizations, taxpayers, and the entire community in the educational process, which is also an integral part of the economic development of the community.
- *The use of leading-edge technologies* to provide communications and linkages among all sectors of the high-performance learning community—school; homes; health, family, and social services; businesses; and community, regional, and national institutions and resources. The learning environment also employs these computer-based technologies in its management and instructional processes.
- *An emphasis on the teacher* as the primary influence in the system. Interdisciplinary teams of educators manage and directly allocate resources for learning as dictated by individual student need. The teacher facilitates learning. Curriculum assessment and human resource development are mutually reinforcing. Training and resources are available to teachers to support their critical role.
- *Provision for a variety of learning settings* that reflect different learning styles, interests, abilities, developmental levels, curriculum requirements, and styles of living.
- *A simulated safe, supportive family-like structure* based on love that provides each student the security of a core of meaningful adults and peers who teach, advise, monitor, relate, and provide service for an extended period of time. This includes referral and access to health, family, and social services.
- *A cohesive management strategy* for individual achievement that is the joint responsibility of the learner, family, and community. There is employee involvement in management functions, and decision making is at the point of production. Trusting relationships exist between managers, employees,

and customers through shared information and cooperation in solving problems and reaching objectives (Marshall, 1991).

Overcoming Resistance

Although nearly all schools would like to say they are restructuring, they are merely applying this label to almost any change program, be it TQM, site-based management, peer conflict resolution, and so on. In truth, most schools remain in a reactive mode, and not one completely reflects the high-performing organization. Many schools have yet even to begin the real creation of this type of community. Some of the reasons why schools are reluctant to undergo systemic and systematic change are identified below:

1. Most school leaders believe they *do* engage in the restructuring effort and that they are actively designing, not adapting to, their futures.
2. Change is uncomfortable. School personnel fear for their job security and prefer not to take risks.
3. School leaders do not understand that creating a high-performance learning community comes from a whole new way of thinking—breaking outworn paradigms. They believe it is enough to plug reform into the existing foundation of the organization.
4. Individuals believe change is too expensive and that there is a lack of funds to support the effort.
5. Stakeholders from all sectors of society are impatient and want to see results immediately, driving leaders to be short-sighted and focused on quick fixes.
6. Schools engage in the rhetoric of the high-performance learning community but fail to mold its culture. They have not made it a priority to hire those who reflect the new order of thinking. The status quo fails to appreciate the high moral commitment and diversity made possible by the employment of more change agents.

The reader is encouraged to explore the extant literature on change, especially the outstanding work of Rosabeth Kanter, to discover ways of overcoming resistance. Some of the strategies that have succeeded for both individuals and teams are listed below:

- Cannibalize recipes of past success.
- Reward unorthodoxy that works.
- Set realistic long-range time lines.
- Inform all sectors of the community of steps to create new systems.
- Make needs known.
- Create the infrastructure to receive such things as grants, equipment, volunteer efforts, and so on.
- Create networks to build trust and enthusiasm based on shared values.
- Collaborate with think tanks that specialize in change, such as the Southwest Regional Educational Laboratories in Austin, Texas.
- Model the high moral commitment, values, and philosophy inherent in a high-performance learning community.
- Hire personnel who reflect the "new organization."

◇2◇

Defining High-Performance Learning Communities

The high-performance learning communities are pragmatic, flexible tools that address curriculum, assessment, staff development, health and social needs, and community involvement. Supported by computer-based technologies—including interactive voice, video, and data—each community can adapt specific design attributes to suit its own needs, resources, and strengths. High-performance learning communities take advantage of existing funding and resources wherever possible, organizing them in new ways that efficiently and effectively assist the learner. In most cases, today's district budgets are sufficient to create the foundation for such a system.

The design of the high-performance learning community encourages active participation by parents, business, and the community and can be used everywhere—rural, suburban, and urban communities. Most importantly, it will offer to all individuals an education that respects their differences, encourages their diversity, and develops them so they will be able to acquire the knowledge and skills necessary to be successful in a 21st-century America.

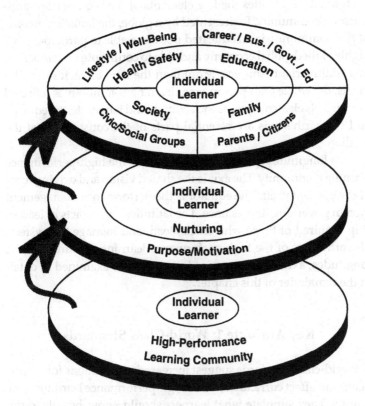

Figure 2.1. The High-Performance Learning Community

Figure 2.1 depicts this learner-centered, community-based, strategically managed nurturing environment. The high-performance learning community will ensure that all individuals learn to their fullest potential. The model promises education, health, and social services to children, their families, and the community. It provides coherence and support for all citizens from birth to death. Through the mastery of specialized skills in preparation for employment at the individual's highest level, learners acquire the abilities and motivation necessary for lifelong learning. In other words, students come to school every day and at every age ready to learn—and they *do* learn.

Figure 2.2 illustrates the key elements of the high-performance learning community. Represented by a globe, the holistic outcome of this community is an educated populace able to participate in a highly skilled global economy and able to contribute to democracy in a multivariant America. More than the sum of each of its elements, the whole high-performance learning community is reflected in each of its elements, just as each latitude and longitude, the equator, and the earth's axis are essential parts of the constitution of the earth.

Each longitude represents an attribute of the high-performance learning community. The axis is the shared vision and driving force of the concept itself. The equator is the performance management system governing its existence. The latitudes are the acts of leadership required of those who create, lead, and manage the system. The attributes of the high-performance learning community (the longitudes, axis, and equator of Figure 2.2) are examined in detail in the remainder of this chapter.

Key Attribute 1: World-Class Standards

World-class standards suggest increased expectations for all students and affect curriculum in the high-performance learning community. They stipulate what learners should know, be able to do, and aspire to be. High standards are intended to replace the current de facto low-level expectations implicit in most current curricula, textbooks, and tests in America. Criteria for quality accompany these standards to provide accountability. These criteria result from competency-based models of outstanding performance such as bench-marking, i.e., examining standards in the finest national and international educational institutions. In addition, instruction, learning, and assessment occur simultaneously within the high-performance curriculum.

Developmental Clusters

To successfully prepare for employment in the global economy, learners progress through four educational stages. Figure 2.3 illus-

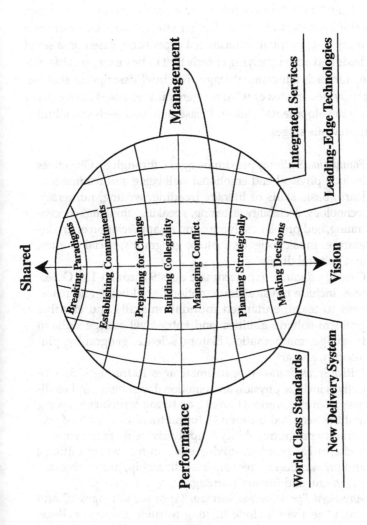

Figure 2.2. Key Elements of the High-Performance Learning Community

trates this progressive sequence of learning experience linked together with flexible transition points. Although age groupings initially broadly define the stages, they are not intended to limit student progress.

The high-performance learning community utilizes the developmental clusters to take the learner from early childhood, through transition, and on to work or further study. Each cluster offers a rich array of appropriate educational experiences based on a set of standards and accompanying criteria that indicate measurable outcomes for each educational stage. The brief description that follows provides an idea of what are generally accepted as objectives of each developmental cluster. Please note that each stage builds upon previous stages.

- *Foundation Skills* (approximate ages 0 through 8). Objectives include physical and emotional well-being and readiness to learn; basic skills of literacy (reading, writing, numeracy, technology, sociability, listening, speaking, thinking, concentrating, and problem solving); and an appreciation of art, literature, music, science, history, geography, social studies, and cultural diversity.
- *General Education* (approximate ages 9 through 15). Objectives include physical and emotional well-being and readiness to learn; enhanced foundation skills and creative problem-solving abilities; and entry-level college skills in language, mathematics, history, science, geography, philosophy, and art.
- *Initial Specialization* (approximate ages 16 through 18). Objectives include physical and emotional well-being and readiness to learn; advanced thinking and creative problem-solving abilities acquired through technical training or college preparatory programs; ability to apply diversified performance and creative problem-solving skills in real-world settings; and preparation for responsible citizenship, productive employment, and further learning.
- *Advanced Specialization Renewal* (approximate ages 19 and up). Objectives include lifelong learning through college, career training, continuing professional education and renewal; and adult literacy.

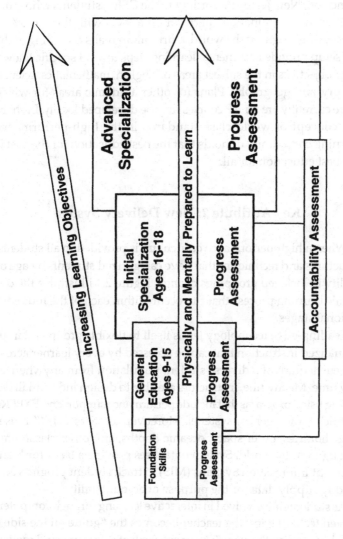

Figure 2.3. Educational Developmental Clusters

15

An Exemplary System

An example that defines academic objectives for achieving high-performance standards is the Advanced Placement (AP) system sponsored by the College Entrance Examination Board (CEEB) in Princeton, New Jersey. According to the CEEB, students who score well on AP examinations perform on a level with the top 5% of students throughout the world. Curriculum plans according to the AP setup provide incremental learning steps toward specific knowledge objectives in the subject areas of English, mathematics, science, history, and geography. Plans for other academic areas for which there currently are no AP courses may be developed locally. In short, the concept of world-class standards in the high-performance learning community upholds that the best education for the best is the best education for all.

Key Attribute 2: New Delivery System

When a high-performance curriculum is provided to all students, structures and techniques that have categorized students by age or ability in lockstep groupings change. Figure 2.4 illustrates the dynamic learning process that can occur within each of the four educational stages.

Leading-edge technology lends itself to flexible group and individualized instruction that can be accessed by every learner across the curriculum of a diverse student population from anywhere at any time. Meanwhile, instructors are able to design individualized pacing using programs that include performance support and EXPERT (artificial intelligence) systems. Moreover, learners "visit" museums, libraries, outer space, oceanic depths, and other classrooms throughout the world. System databases provide a basis for Management Information Systems (MIS) to track student progress and readily supply data for the purpose of accountability.

As students are involved in interactive learning through computer-driven technologies, the teacher becomes the "guide on the side," not the "sage on the stage"; he or she facilitates learning and models

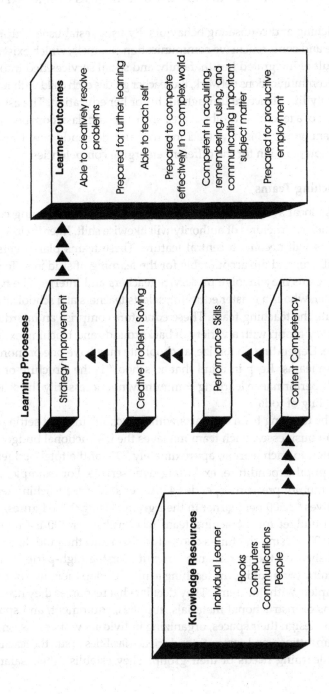

Learning Processes

Strategy Improvement

Creative Problem Solving

Performance Skills

Content Competency

Learner Outcomes

Able to creatively resolve problems

Prepared for further learning

Able to teach self

Prepared to compete effectively in a complex world

Competent in acquiring, remembering, using, and communicating important subject matter

Prepared for productive employment

Knowledge Resources

Individual Learner

Books
Computers
Communications
People

Figure 2.4. Learning Processes

17

coaching and counseling behaviors. By using established supportive and comprehensive communication channels, which exist as a result of integrated health, family, and social services tied into the telecommunications network, the teacher guides each child within this family-like structure throughout his or her education. The assignment of a teacher to a subject area and a specific classroom becomes meaningless. This new teaching role also demands new training and preparation for the different emerging competencies.

Teaching Teams

As local systems design their high-performance learning communities, structures of authority will likewise shift. Interdisciplinary teams will become a central feature. These teams plan, oversee, facilitate, and are accountable for the learning of students. Teaching teams may involve preservice teachers and interns. The team leader, who is a master educator, selects teachers at a school site to create the teaching team. These educators comprise an interdisciplinary group with a variety of backgrounds and teaching experience. Depending on its size, a school site may have one or more of these teams. Keep in mind that a "school" is the structure of the high-performance learning community, not necessarily the school building of today.

The teaching team contracts with the school, in effect setting up small businesses. Each team manages the instructional budget allocated to each learner, approximately 70% of the total budgeted per-pupil expenditure, excluding debt service. For example, if a community presently spends $4,000 per student, a teaching team receives $2,800 per learner in their group. Using these figures, the total budget for a teaching team responsible for 100 learners is $280,000. Using the funds allotted to them and the guidelines established by the governance structure for the high-performance learning community, the teaching teams develop their own budget complete with line items. They decide what resources they need in terms of instructional materials, supplies, equipment, and space. They design their spaces, organizing individual work areas, small group settings, and computer and science facilities to suit the teaching and learning needs of their group. They establish their salaries with options for incentives for achieving agreed-on outcomes determined by the team leader and the governance structure. How well learners achieve curricular objectives is the critical factor of a teaching team's success. Lastly, teaching teams make personnel decisions, such as hiring support staff and recruiting parents and community volunteers.

Team Leader

Depending on conditions at each school site, a single leader will likely represent all the teams, especially in the beginning. He or she will be responsible to the team for coordinating overarching activities and processes. This duty may be in addition to those obligations already performed as a member of a teaching team. A team leader is usually responsible for the following activities:

- Providing leadership to the teaching teams
- Coordinating the overall administrative and support functions of the site, including budget coordination and record keeping
- Assigning children to teaching teams
- Setting standards and determines outcomes
- Managing school purchasing
- Evaluating the progress of the teaching teams through the performance management system. (See Key Attribute 6)
- Coordinating human resources at the site

Community Involvement

Parents and citizens participate in the overall social development and academic learning of students along with the teaching teams. They serve as part-time teachers, mentors, and aides. Every child has a mentor or support person who knows the child and his or her family. The goal is to prevent a student from falling between the cracks. Parents and citizens have the responsibility to maintain contact with families through the telecommunications network and social activities. The high-performance learning community encourages all parents to become active participants in their child's education.

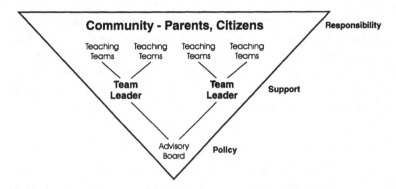

Figure 2.5. Governance for the High-Performance Learning Community

Each teaching team has professional support, such as access to technology staff to assist with equipment and training. Members also have the support of social workers, health care providers, and other human service professionals who are responsible for diagnosing and making referrals to the necessary support services that guarantee student academic success.

In consultation with the team leader, parents, and social service providers, teaching teams are responsible for the discipline of students within their group. The community together develops standards for behavior, working collaboratively to develop rules and guidelines.

Each site has an advisory board or governance structure composed of parents and members of the community. The advisory board takes an active role in the management of the site, setting policy, and establishing support mechanisms. However, governance remains a key responsibility of teaching teams as depicted in Figure 2.5.

A Showcase Example

Ochoa Elementary School in Tucson, Arizona, is a showcase for the new community-based delivery system. Existing beyond the type of community involvement typical of many schools, it exemplifies community inclusion. The principal, teachers, and parents are members of a single team. Together, they create, modify, and implement changes in the school's culture. They have redefined their school as a community responsible for setting and reaching its own goals and capable of managing its own resources.

The school is accountable, in part, to a coalition of parents and community members. These individuals engage in intensive professional development and reflection, and sponsor training opportunities for the entire community. The coalition has several subcommittees dedicated to quality of life issues, such as the integration of health and human services, safety, and extended care.

The teaching team is continuously involved in action research. Classes are no longer divided by age or the students' language proficiency. Monolingual (i.e., English or Spanish) students of all ages are combined with bilingual students of all ages and taught by teachers who are certified in both languages. The team also uses innovative techniques to teach traditional subjects in the context of students' everyday lives. Students engage in community projects as learning experiences.

American schools can no longer excel with the standardized curriculum, delivered by standardized classroom practices, producing a standardized product. The attribute of a new delivery system, more than any other key element of the high-performance learning community, engages the most creative educators, maximizes their capabilities, and optimizes their contributions. To guarantee that all children achieve world-class standards, the teacher harnesses the necessary resources from the community, in accordance with the student's individual needs, to make that goal possible.

Key Attribute 3: Integrated Services

America's need to develop a specialized workforce that is competent to function in a global economy has pressured educators to elevate student performance. Currently, most schools receive students impacted by severe social and economic conditions that affect their readiness to learn and their ability to sustain academic pursuits. Schools nationwide have long realized that it is nearly impossible to educate children whose lives are in chaos due to poverty, hunger, abuse, malnutrition, ill health, family disintegration, homelessness, neglect, fear, and hopelessness. Although school systems may be the only one reliable contact for troubled children and their families, they are powerless on their own to alleviate the chaos.

In the present social service delivery system, at-risk children and their families must use their own initiative to seek out appropriate resources. Services are organized, funded, and staffed to deal with human problems in separate buildings and by separate agencies, programs, and professionals. By contrast, the high-performance learning community uses a community-based integrated delivery system to serve mutual clients. This collaborative network, sometimes referred to as "one-stop shopping" or "the full-service school," has fluid, permeable boundaries.

The high-performance learning community addresses the health, safety, family, and living needs of its learners. It focuses on the well-being of children and nurtures them through a simulated family environment. *Well-being* is the condition of being well, i.e., happy, free from fear and unusual anxiety; it is the ability to survive. The concentration of community resources to support the physical, intellectual, emotional, social, and spiritual needs of children, i.e., the whole child, is in actuality a call to reconstitute the notion of civic life.

The leadership of the local high-performance learning community—housed in the team leader and advisory board—draws community agencies and businesses into a unitary, cooperative effort solely for the well-being of learners. This supportive environment fosters the maximum development of a person from before birth through childhood to adulthood. It gives coherency and rationality to what has been a collection of fragmented services, allowing a more efficient and effective allocation of resources. After all, education is the critical factor in the quality of life for all Americans.

In other words, all forces within a community serve the best interests of children so that each learner will attain high-performance standards by maximizing resources. In order to accomplish its collective mission more humanely and effectively, each high-performance learning community has embedded within it a voluntary referral system that links the school site with health, family, social service providers, and other critical community and regional support services (Cunningham, 1990). Rather than increase staff beyond feasible funding levels, or duplicate services at one or more sites, telecommunications connect the children and their families with available resources. This collaborative network provides discernible, distinct benefits leading to academic success and guarantees the delivery of services from providers to multiple learners and their families as dictated by each learner's needs. Should a child have numerous and interconnected problems, as is often the case, the delivery of integrated services eliminates costly overlap of efforts. Most importantly, such a system allows teachers to be educators rather than parents, nurses, social workers, counselors, nutritionists, and the multitudinous other roles that teachers typically play.

Model "Full-Service" School

Santa Rosa County, Florida, has "full-service" schools that integrate educational, medical, and social services for children and their families on school grounds or in other easily accessible locations. A concentrated effort is made to eliminate duplication through the relocation or reallocation of available services. A software interrelational database program is critical to the project's success. This program organizes and coordinates all data related to each student so that information can be shared among different groups providing assistance to students and their families. The county has engaged in this project for 5 years, and research shows increases in learning, personal effectiveness, and efficiency; an increase in clients placed in jobs; a reduction in problems related to health, behavior, truancy, drugs, and alcohol; and a reduction in self-injurious behaviors and criminal offenses.

This example demonstrates the increased capability of teachers when they receive the support services they need from health, family, and social services providers. Indeed, the African proverb is well-taken here: "It takes a whole village to raise a child."

Key Attribute 4: Leading-Edge Technologies

It is only through the full integration of technology that the high-performance learning community can become a reality. Technology serves three primary purposes in the high-performance learning community: (a) a tool in the instructional process, (b) a tool to manage information, and (c) a communications mechanism.

Technology in Instruction

Technology is truly a catalyst to learning. Today, most instructional software is used to directly support classroom instruction. Albeit a limited use of instructional technology, this can not only promote interest and curiosity but, most importantly, makes available an enlarged window to the universe. With technology as a vehicle, learners can (a) access and create information; (b) discover and explore relationships, concepts, and places; (c) use information for deductions, decision making, and problem solving; and (d) communicate with others anywhere in the world and at any time. One of the greatest areas for application is in the instruction and rehabilitation of handicapped learners. Technology enables all learners to receive appropriate instruction on any subject no matter where they are located and at the time they desire or need it.

Instructional designers have the challenge to develop programs to meet learners' individual needs, interests, abilities, pace, learning styles, and living styles. Powerful databases, which may be located anywhere, can be accessed through the use of networks to open new worlds of knowledge. A wide range of available databases holds enough information to allow a student to clarify questions, study an issue in depth, or branch out to new subjects. For example, through interactive video disks (IVD), a student can tour the Louvre and ask questions about one or more of the treasures housed there. Numerous books, articles, and other library materials for the study of any subject can also be accessed on CD-ROM disks. The artificial intelligence technology in EXPERT systems lets students repair a jet engine or perform numerous other operations that require technical knowledge and skill likely beyond the expertise of their teacher. A learner can instantaneously communicate with anyone anywhere through electronic mail. Satellite instruction, sponsored by a growing number of private or public sector organizations and universities, encourages students to participate with other learners located throughout the world.

Technology in Management Applications and Communication

Technology is designed to include systems for electronic storage and transfer of data about students, such as assessments, health, and family statistics. Those requiring use of these files for decision making and problem solving can access them as needed, regardless of location. Responsible individuals can efficiently enter reports that are instantaneously available without the interference and labor that so often accompanies such activities. In fact, all partners in a strategically managed high-performance learning community may communicate about a particular student, issue, or problem wherever and whenever the need to share information emerges. Hence, everyone involved is kept informed about the learner's academic progress, behavior, and other areas of mutual interest to the learner through this critical function of the storage and transferral of data.

Whatever one can imagine in terms of the delivery of instruction, the management of information, and communication can happen with technology. Electronic products and services continue to decrease in cost and are an excellent means to reduce the effects of a decaying system of financial support and infrastructures. For relatively little expenditure, students can own a laptop computer and modem to access the universe. Students construct their own learning projects and find the sources of information they require for successful completion of their work. On-line assistance for learners is available as needed—24 hours per day from anywhere—facilitating collaboration among teachers, students, and the community around the world.

Examples of Technology at Work

Plano Independent School District in Plano, Texas, relies on computer-based technologies for the teaching-learning process.

The District is currently engaged in a project to introduce technology throughout all subject areas of the curriculum for grades K-5. The teachers are involved with Edunetics Corporation, Arlington, Virginia, in developing the curriculum. They primarily prescribe content while Edunetics contributes the technological expertise. At the same time, Edunetics provides a teacher training component and offers continued customer support. The technology incorporates a variety of tools, including databases, spreadsheets, lessons, and third-party software. In addition, the school district employs technology throughout the instructional process, helping every student to master the curriculum.

Another example of what the new technologies can contribute to the reinvention of the educational system is seen in Indian River, Florida. Three years ago the superintendent of schools led a project to achieve lifelong learning as the basis of personal and economic growth, social development, and community problem solving. He employed community-wide telecomputing as a strategy to attain the goal, calling it the Indian River Electronic Network for Education (IRENE). Today, nearly 18 schools and neighborhoods with over 20,000 homes, 3,000 businesses, community centers, churches, libraries, and health and human services agencies are linked for learning dedicated to developing self-directed, cooperative students of all ages—preschoolers to senior citizens. IRENE is also linked to Internet. Since IRENE's implementation, students' demands on the network for more educational programs have increased, and television viewing by students has decreased by 40%.

Using the efficiencies of technology, the high-performance learning community guarantees each learner academic success as a natural part and process of civic life. Technological tools assist students, their parents, educators, and community-based organizations in designing a plan unique to each learner's comprehensive needs. By addressing growth in all dimensions—physical, intellectual, social, emotional, and spiritual—those who use technology in instruction, management, and communication can vastly increase the quality of our education. Although technology does not transform schooling in and of itself, it supports and sustains the planning, implementation, management, and evaluation of the high-performance learning community (see Figure 2.6).

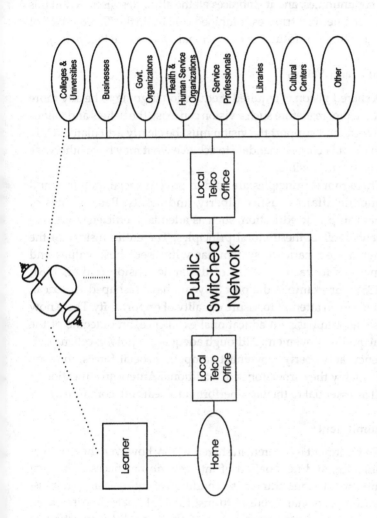

Figure 2.6. New Information Technology System

Colleges & Universities

Businesses

Govt. Organizations

Health & Human Service Organizations

Service Professionals

Libraries

Cultural Centers

Other

Local Telco Office

Public Switched Network

Local Telco Office

Learner

Home

27

Key Attribute 5: Shared Vision

Shared vision is the driving force behind high-performance learning communities, and it embraces all the attributes discussed in this chapter. The six attributes combined constitute the "lived ethic" of the new high-performance educational system (see Figure 2.2).

Beliefs and Values

A shared vision is required if education is going to be any more than mediocre. Before such a vision can exist, the beliefs and values that form and support the vision must be clearly articulated. Only then can it become a mandate to achieve what may have otherwise appeared impossible.

Three moral principles are said to govern social, political, and economic affairs—justice, liberty, and equity. Basic values of American public education, such as adequacy, efficiency, and excellence, reflect these moral principles. The entire history of the American educational system has witnessed these values and principles in various states of dynamic tension (Adler, 1981, p. 135). For example, the past 30 years have reshaped American schools in an attempt to assure equality of opportunity. There now exists an emphasis on educational excellence, an outcome of the total quality movement. Although adequacy, equity, excellence, efficiency, and liberty may enlist competing social forces, they are undeniably the cornerstones of traditional American education as well as essential to the high-performance learning community.

Commitment

Commitment is inherent in shared vision; however, rhetoric, manipulation, and negotiation of interests do not necessarily elicit commitment. Commitment is a condition of enthusiasm that transfers from personal interests to institutional goals; it arises from consciously accepted moral values linked to goal-driven action. In this way, shared values, aligned with organizational purposes, drive shared vision as enthusiasm spreads within a community. Once the organization identifies its foundation values and beliefs and is able to come to consensus, it then derives purpose. Having purpose, the organization can write that shared vision based on the underlying values that define its mission. The "lived ethic" of the shared vision then forms the basis of all decisions. In the high-performance learning community, elements that sustain shared vision include moral principles, beliefs, values, purpose, dedication of time and effort, development of feeling and passion, and the establishment of focus.

With a shared dream of what education can become, goals take on a new meaning. This marks the birth of a holistic community that is more than the sum of its parts. Members move toward its creation by means of long- and short-term goals. Achieving these goals yields the reality of a learner-centered, community-based, strategically managed high-performance educational system.

Key Attribute 6: Performance Management

Performance management is central to the high-performance learning community, just as the equator is at the center of the earth's systems (see Figure 2.2). Performance management provides a model for unifying and improving the management of resources; processes; individual, group, and organization performance; and educational quality. It is synonymous with continuous improvement or Total Quality Management. Figure 2.7, Managing High Performance, illustrates the three "wheels" of the process. The intention engine reflects the shared vision, complete with its commitment and high moral principles that generate the power for performance management—strategic planning, goal setting, tactical planning, policy making, implementation, and assessment and evaluation. In turn, the desired results wheel indicates the outcome of accountability measures. A performance management system is imperative to help students achieve mastery in the high-performance learning community.

Figure 2.8 illustrates the Performance Management System and depicts (a) the resources, or inputs; (b) the processes of the system; and (c) the outcomes. These are the metasystems that constitute a

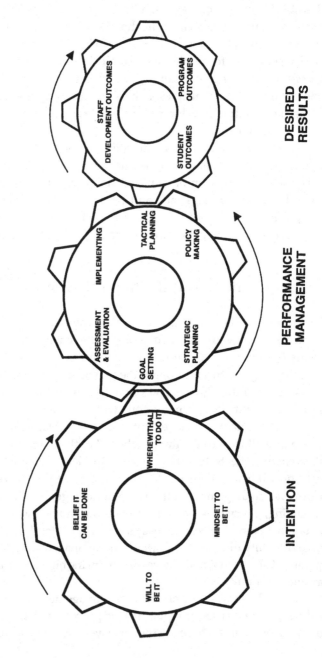

Figure 2.7. Managing High Performance

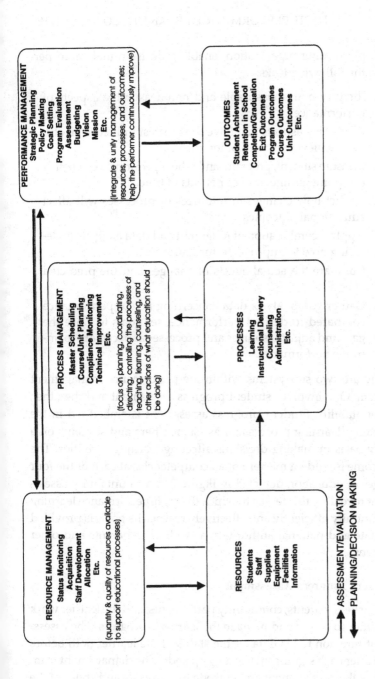

PERFORMANCE MANAGEMENT
Strategic Planning
Policy Making
Goal Setting
Program Evaluation
Assessment
Budgeting
Vision
Mission
Etc.

(Integrate & unify management of resources, processes, and outcomes; help the performer continuously improve)

OUTCOMES
Student Achievement
Retention in School
Completion/Graduation
Exit Outcomes
Program Outcomes
Course Outcomes
Unit Outcomes
Etc.

PROCESS MANAGEMENT
Master Scheduling
Course/Unit Planning
Compliance Monitoring
Technical Improvement
Etc.

(focus on planning, coordinating, directing, controlling the processes of teaching, learning, counseling, and other actions of what education should be doing)

PROCESSES
Learning
Instructional Delivery
Counseling
Administration
Etc.

RESOURCE MANAGEMENT
Status Monitoring
Acquisition
Staff Development
Allocation
Etc.

(quantity & quality of resources available to support educational processes)

RESOURCES
Students
Staff
Supplies
Equipment
Facilities
Information

ASSESSMENT/EVALUATION
PLANNING/DECISION MAKING

Figure 2.8. Performance Management System

31

high-performing organization, enabling decision makers to perform the following tasks:

1. Identify both measurable and nonmeasurable aspects of performance.
2. Determine aspects that have the greatest influence on student achievement and other outcomes.
3. Measure student, program, and school performance, whether at a point in time or over periods of time.
4. Predict how changes in resources or processes will affect educational outcomes.
5. Apply a combination of judgment and data analysis in deciding how to improve performance.
6. Compare the actual effects of changes and the predicted effects
7. Gather gap analysis data concerning actual performance compared to desired performance, set goals to close the gap, and adjust resources and processes as necessary to improve performance.

There are two subsystems within the performance management system. One involves student progress assessment and the other, accountability. Student progress assessment is embedded in the teaching/learning process and assists teachers and students on a daily basis in making decisions affecting learning activities. The outcome is student mastery of all competencies at each of the four stages of education depicted in Figure 2.3. Accountability assessment revealing the degree to which the high-performance learning community efficiently and effectively reaches its goals is provided to state and national authorities, as well as to parents and other citizens.

Student Progress Assessment

Teachers, parents, community participants, and the learner work together to assess and manage the learner's progress. The assessment function holds data on the status of the learner both before and after each significant learning episode. The management team tailors the environment and episode to the needs and styles of the learner. The teaching team orchestrates the learning process so that

Learning Processes	Item Tests	Performance Tasks	Student Exhibits	Process Measures
Strategy Improvement	Low	Medium	Medium	High
Creative Problem Solving	Low	Medium	High	High
Performance Skills	Low	High	Medium	High
Subject Matter Competency	High	Medium	Low	Low
	Current Assessment Practice		Enhanced Assessment Practice	

Figure 2.9. Testing Instruments

the learner achieves each and every desired outcome. The learning episode might be a short lesson, a team project, or one entire year of learning. The model is appropriate for each type of episode, but the types of assessment methods used vary according to the type, the completion time, and the skill being developed.

The teaching team uses multiple instruments to assess learner progress including item tests; performance tests; student exhibits or demonstrations; process measurements or assessments, e.g., portfolios; interviews; and questionnaires. Figure 2.9 compares current assessment practices to the enhanced practices used in the high-performance learning community. It shows the types of instruments that have the highest validity for assessing the acquisition of subject matter competency and for developing performance skills, creative problem-solving abilities, and advanced learning strategies.

Process assessment methods blur the distinction between assessment and instruction; i.e., learning occurs during assessment, and assessment occurs as a by-product of learning. Daily progress assessment relies less on standard item tests than on the interaction of adults with students. This learning process reveals whether or not students really know what they say they know or really understand the salient concepts. Cooperative learning episodes involve students in integrated performance and creative problem-solving projects, taking into account the quality of the assessment processes as well as the quality of the end results. These projects form the basis for the high-performance, multidisciplinary curriculum that relies on the assessment practices most suitable for the tasks being performed.

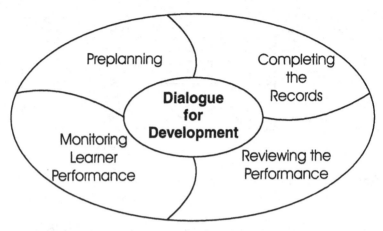

Figure 2.10. Student Progress Assessment Model

Teachers rarely use item tests because their use often disrupts the flow of a learning activity, disengaging the student from productive learning. When the teaching team does use item tests, the environment is stress free, and learners are not in danger of receiving "failing" grades. In the best sense, item tests are indicators of how much progress a student has made and how much more he or she needs to learn. These tests are used to detect areas of misunderstanding or the need for further study. They also provide information for the planning of follow-up activities.

Dialogue for Development is the best model for the successful conferencing between the teaching team and the learner, a process integral to the high-performance learning community. The name itself suggests the active participation of the learner in the assessment process in which teachers and students are equal partners. Figure 2.10 illustrates the four successive stages of the Student Progress Assessment Model—preplanning, completing the records, reviewing the performance, and monitoring learner performance.

The first stage, preplanning, provides the opportunity for the teaching team to prepare the learner for the assessment and gather the data relevant to the student's performance.

The second stage, completing the records, allows for the teaching team to rate each learner's current progress according to the standards and criteria established between the team and the learner for a particular learning episode. This progress information is called a performance plan or the individual educational plan and is mutually determined at the previous conference. At this time the teaching team also prepares a performance plan for the next learning episode. It may contain the following: goals; objectives or competencies; activities or behavioral indicators that include criteria and standards; responsibilities of all those involved in the students' development at this particular time including the teaching team, parents, and community support members such as nurses, psychologists, and nutritionists; time line; and validation, i.e., the form of assessment. The management information system of the high-performance learning community can record and track this data, making it easily accessible to all parties involved in the education and development of the learner.

Following preplanning and record completion, the teaching team and student meet for the third stage, the performance review. The meeting may not necessarily be face-to-face but may take place through the use of telecommunications. This is the time for student feedback regarding his or her progress and the next performance plan. It is an excellent opportunity for both the teaching team and student to clarify roles and expectations.

Monitoring learner performance is the fourth stage and takes place throughout the execution of the learner's performance plan. The teaching team is readily accessible to give feedback in accordance with their responsibilities and validation of the plan. All parties may update the performance plan as necessary. The use of technology makes this process most efficient and keeps the focus on the development of the learner.

Figure 2.11, Managing Student Progress Assessment, uses the same configuration as Figure 2.8 to depict the student assessment subsystem. It illustrates the status of resources before the learning episode, the instructional process itself, and the outcomes or student gains resulting from his or her experience in the learning episode.

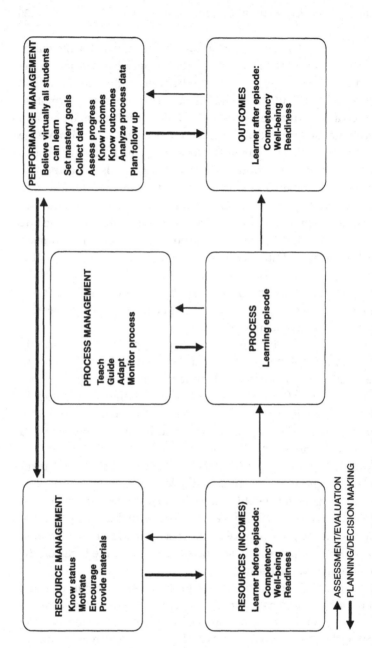

Figure 2.11. Managing Student Progress Assessment

Accountability Assessment

Accountability assessment, the second component of the Performance Management System, holds students accountable for their behavior and performance—by their teachers, their parents, their school site, and their community. Actually, everyone in the high-performance learning community is accountable. Parents are held accountable by their children, their children's teachers, their children's school site, and their communities; the school site is held accountable by its students, teachers, parents of the students, and its community; and the community is held accountable by its students, its parents, its teachers, and its school sites. In other words, each of the key groups in the community of learners holds accountable each of the other key groups. Because each group is a valued customer of the other groups, it provides feedback regarding how efficiently and effectively they are supported.

Accountability assessment depends upon the use of a results-oriented evaluation method that can determine the degree of attainment of the goals for which a learning process was initiated. For the high-performance learning community, accountability assessment emphasizes the effectiveness of the education system, i.e., to what degree all learners achieve high-performance standards or to what degree an educational system upholds shared values.

Computer-based technologies support the functions of performance planning and assessment, data collection, data analysis, and report generation. Performance measurement data stored and managed electronically serve as the primary source of accountability and progress. With technology, there is also the immense capability to transfer this data from one source to another. The computerized management system assists managers in quickly detecting and diagnosing performance problems within the learning environment and provides easy access to information needed for decision making.

In summary, this system serves several functions: (a) It gives parents, teachers, and learners better information concerning student progress; (b) it gives advisory board members the capability to assess the performance of their learning community relative to its own past performances; and (c) it gives all parties involved in the educational process of the community the ability to assess their performance relative to other high-performance communities. In addition, the performance management system becomes a source from which citizens can retrieve accountability data for evaluations, including the analysis of policies affecting student achievement, according to the shared vision. Perhaps most importantly, it keeps detailed stories of past performance so that high-performance learning communities can set realistic goals from which to achieve high levels of effectiveness.

Preparing Leaders for the New Learning Communities

Historians report that leadership is America's scarcest resource and, as such, is the primary reason our country falls further behind in efforts to regain prominence in today's economic and cultural world. This lack of leadership exists in both the public and private sectors and does not exempt the area of education. At the same time, leadership and its accompanying transformative power is what is needed to achieve the reconstitution of American education. This chapter evolves around the kind of leadership and change strategies required to establish high-performance learning communities. The following discussion treats two topics:

1. The competencies, including the knowledge base, leadership acts, and performance skills needed to create, lead, and manage high-performance learning communities
2. The training program designed to provide potential leaders with the necessary knowledge and skills for such a task

Competencies

Variations in job performance result from the degree of profiency with which individuals execute certain critical tasks on the job. A *critical task* is a behavior that is (a) considered important by peers, supervisors, and subordinates; (b) has a wide variation among its performers; and (c) allows this variability to be easily perceived by others. The degree to which an individual performs a critical task well is a function of the degree of mastery and integration or coordination of the component knowledge and skills involved to produce the desired result. Component knowledge and skills are competencies. In the study of exemplary performance, researchers investigate subjects who have demonstrated performance success on the critical factors for their particular role. What results from this study is a competency model or performance profile that is used to develop educational programs in a curriculum designed to train individuals for a particular role (see Resource B).

Educational research reveals that the superintendent's leadership is the single most important factor in creating a positive district ethos with both cultural and technical factors contributing to its success (Coleman and Larocque, 1988). However, researchers have only studied an exceptionally small sample of exemplary performing superintendents and principals who have significantly impacted student outcomes. In addition, no true high-performance learning community sufficiently exhibiting all six attributes currently exists. The consequent inability to study successful leaders in the high-performance learning community in general is a significant drawback. Instructional designers have developed a curriculum for the high-performance learning community by constructing a leadership competency model by means of a job/tasks/function analysis of actions that constitute the six essential attributes—establishing world-class standards; adapting, reorganizing, and inventing a new delivery system; integrating health, family, and social services; employing leading-edge technologies; creating a shared vision; and building a performance management system. To supplement the job/tasks/function analysis, they have also referred to relevant competencies already substantiated in the literature such as the work of Harris and Wan (1991) and the American Association of School Administrators (AASA) Educational Administrator Effectiveness Profile (1988). The acts of leadership that emerged from this process include breaking paradigms, establishing commitment, preparing for change, building collegiality, managing conflict, planning strategically, and making decisions (see also Figure 2.2 and Resource B). The performance skills needed by leaders of high-performance learning communities are as follows: communication skills (oral and written), facilitating skills, ability to gain strength through a diversity of skills, ability to develop skills of self and staff, and marketing skills. This competency model will remain unvalidated until school officials establish true high-performance learning communities.

Training Programs

There appears to be increasing public discontent concerning our nation's educational administration programs, and there is persistent clamor for reform. The discontent rests in the belief that status quo ideologies are inadequate and in the lack of clinical experiences. The rising fury regarding the ineptitude of the American public school system paves the way for the implementation of innovative training programs.

Instructional designers have developed a competency-driven curriculum to prepare potential school leaders to create, lead, and manage high-performance learning communities. Three content areas are featured: (a) the knowledge base of the high-performance learning community based on the six attributes; (b) the acts of leadership; and (c) the performance skills. The curriculum incorporates the components of sound instructional design: The content is performance based, not subject matter based; activities are recursive, interactive, and include opportunity for self-assessment. In addition, the curriculum involves practical applications in real educational settings. The training program, including on-the-job practice, takes

2 years from start to finish. One such program resides at the University of Texas at Austin in the College of Education.

Effective leadership development can occur only when individuals acknowledge their knowledge, skill, and ability deficiencies as they exist between their actual performance and desired performance. To do this, the participants use 360° instruments that measure an individual's performance in several dimensions by three categories of ratings—self, subordinate, and superior. The assessment measures the participant's degree of strength in the competencies required of leaders of high-performance learning communities.

Integral to the success of training programs is a curriculum that is recursive, i.e., participants do what they see and hear. For example, an attribute of a high-performance learning community is to attain mastery reflective of certain world-class standards. Consequently, participants, upon completion of each of the modules of the training program, demonstrate the following high-performance competencies in a variety of culminating activities (see Lesson Plan below):

1. *Break outmoded organizational paradigms* by visioning, planning strategically, and managing change.
2. *Establish the high-performance paradigm* that is built on the values of love expressed in community, excellence in achievement, and liberty through the realization of potential, equity of opportunity, adequacy of resources, and efficiency for the public interest. The high-performance learning community exemplifies the following attributes: (a) world-class standards, (b) new delivery systems, (c) integrated services, (d) leading-edge technologies, (e) shared vision, and (f) performance management.
3. *Establish world-class standards* that ensure all learners are equipped with the knowledge and skills required to compete successfully in a high-skill, high-wage economy.
   • Transform the current educational system into a community-based, learner-centered, strategically managed, nurturing environment that enables all individuals to learn to their fullest potential.

- Adapt, reorganize, and invent delivery systems based upon the intensive utilization of educational and tele-communications technologies that foster communications, provide information, and allow access to community, regional, national, and international resources.
- Integrate health, family, social, and business services that all learners can access to create a nurturing environment.
- Employ leading-edge technologies to manage and deliver curriculum, student assessment and accountability processes, and services that work in concert to assure the access to necessary resources for the well-being of each individual learner.
- Share the vision to build the new notion of civic life, via collaborative networks.
- Implement a performance management system, emphasizing student progress assessment and program accountability and incorporating the principles of total quality management and continuous process improvement. Learners, parents, teachers, and the community are accountable to each other for the goals of the high-performance learning community.

4. *Build commitment* within oneself and others—a commitment that is based on strong moral conviction concerning significant social purposes.

5. *Create a professional community* characterized by high commitment, competence, and autonomy that works collaboratively to effect system transformation.

6. *Prepare for change* through (a) evaluating the need for change, (b) defining the future state, (c) describing the present state, (d) assessing the present in terms of the future, (e) planning for change, (f) conducting the appropriate intervention(s) that facilitates complex system change, (g) managing the transition, (h) stabilizing the change, and (i) evaluating the change.

7. *Plan strategically* by (a) transforming the conventional bureaucratic paradigm, (b) sharing the vision with all stakeholders and aligning their collaborative support, (c)

strategically and systematically conducting the planning process, and (d) influencing effectively.

8. *Improve decision-making skills* through problem identification, decision factoring, and potential problem analysis.

9. *Develop conflict management capabilities* that manage power dynamics, communicate across cultures, gain strength through diversity, and generate healing and reconciliation among parties.

10. *Build collegiality* through developing norms of self-acceptance, respect for individual differences, giving and receiving feedback, solving problems, letting go of the past, and celebrating the accomplishments of the present. These norms focus on both task and relationship behaviors.

Recursive design is also used to make the attribute of performance management an integral part of the curriculum. Instructors begin each lesson with the student progress assessment for that particular learning episode, practicing the Dialogue for Development model as appropriate. The session concludes with a culminating activity in which participants demonstrate *all* the competencies of that particular lesson. They are joined by their classmates and the instructors in determining their mastery of the competencies.

In addition, recursive design is the provision of a nurturing environment enhanced through the integration of community services to guarantee each participant's success in mastering the competencies. The expectation is that each participant masters every competency. There is no failure; everyone passes to the next step as instructors provide developmental assistance in accordance with an individual's needs until 100% mastery is achieved.

Instructors use multiple methods, accompanied by a variety of media, to guarantee active participation in a successful training program. Methods to elicit high involvement include lecturette, demonstration, observation, visitation, case study, guided imagery, instrumentation, role play, games and simulation, research, field study, and independent reading. Media include print materials, such as the participant guides; audio materials, such as voice and audio tapes; projected materials, such as flip charts, transparencies, and videos; and three-dimensional objects, such as magic tricks. In a 4-hour session, the lecturette format occupies only 25% or less of the time. Teamwork is a focal point for activity. Some projects require the same team members to work together throughout the 2-year period, whereas other projects allow for randomly assembled teams. Some teams are as small as two members, and some are as large as eight. The training group itself consists of 16 members.

Lesson Plan

A sample lesson plan follows. It features a half-day-long module on Shared Vision, which is a knowledge-based unit of the curriculum. Shared Vision is one of the six attributes of the high-performance learning community. The module at a glance is followed by an overview of various processes that participants use in learning the content constituting the lesson.

THE MODULE AT A GLANCE

Course: 2-year curriculum for creating, leading, and managing a high-performance learning community (HPLC)

Unit: Shared Vision

Module: Sharing the Vision

Time: 4 hours (1/2 day)

Facility: One room large enough to accommodate:
— U-shaped tables and chairs for 16 participants
— Small group work areas for four teams
Break-out rooms for small group work for two teams

Objectives (Participant)

1. Define shared vision.
2. Describe the attributes of a shared vision.
3. Identify the behaviors necessary to creating a shared vision.

4. Use the strategic planning process to formulate values or beliefs and purpose.
5. Develop one's personal vision and a shared vision.
6. Identify the obstacles to creating a shared vision.
7. Write an action plan for the reduction/elimination of obstacles in creating a shared vision.
8. Define symbolic leadership.

We Want Leaders Who: Commit to a shared vision of the HPLC.

Align their own personal vision with the shared vision of the HPLC.

Create a shared vision of the HPLC.

Manage the development of a shared vision of the HPLC.

Demonstrate their role as symbolic transformational leaders.

Who Can: Determine the "lived ethic" of their organization.

Develop the purpose of their organization based on the lived ethic.

Articulate the shared vision of the HPLC.

Align support for the shared vision of the HPLC.

Significant Outcomes: A shared vision founded in a lived ethic that determines the purpose of education. In other words, a shared vision of HPLC.

Culminating Demonstration: Participants will create a shared vision of the HPLC that is founded in the lived ethic and in their role as moral agents and symbolic and transformational leaders. They will each write an action plan emphasizing the behaviors necessary to create a shared vision and reduce or eliminate the obstacles to the shared vision of the HPLC.

Agenda

Pretraining Package (includes readings and activities)	4 hours
Module Introduction	35 minutes
Activity #1: Shared Vision	15 minutes
Lecturette: Shared Vision	15 minutes
Activity #2: Small Group Consensus	65 minutes
Lecturette: The Symbolic Leader	15 minutes
Activity #3: Helping Trios	65 minutes
Module Conclusion	30 minutes

Instructional Methodology:
- Lecturette
- Small group experience
- Case study
- Instrumentation
- Independent study

Equipment:
- Overhead projector
- Flipchart, easel, and markers (six sets)
- Masking tape (five rolls)
- Pointer

Instructor Materials:
- Transparencies #1-7
- Flipchart #1
- *Leader's Guide*

Participant Materials:
- *Participant Guide* (16)
- Pretraining Package (16 sets)

PROCESS OVERVIEW

Analyze

- Analyze the difference between a personal vision and a shared vision.
- Determine the behaviors of the transformational symbolic leader as they pertain to a shared vision.

- Examine the obstacles to a shared vision and determine ways to overcome them.
- Develop values for the greater society that demonstrate their role as a moral agent with care for others and responsibility for themselves.
- Assess the purpose in the culture of high-performing systems.
- Evaluate one's own educational beliefs, values, and mission.

Apply

- Create one's personal vision.
- Determine values or beliefs using the format for building values derived from a strategic planning conference.
- Formulate a mission or purpose statement for schooling.
- Share one's vision with others and solicit their reactions; examine one's vision in terms of its congruence with a "lived ethic"; refine as appropriate to create a shared vision.
- Identify strategies and establish a personal action plan to reduce and/or overcome the obstacles to the shared vision of the HPLC.

Synthesize

- Review and articulate the role and responsibilities of the leader in creating a shared vision.
- Draft a personal shared vision that will describe what each segment of the educational community will "see" when that vision is reality.
- Review and articulate the process of purposing in a high-performance system.

Translations

- Define vision.
- Define shared vision.
- Identify the critical attributes of vision.
- Identify the components of shared vision.
- Review and reflect upon identified literature and research.

Terms

- Lived ethic
- Vision
- Moral agent
- Symbolic leadership
- Transformational leader
- Purposing
- Sacred authority
- Shared vision
- Culture
- Values
- Beliefs
- Mission

Procedures

- Planning
- Discussing
- Analyzing
- Reflecting
- Facilitating
- Mission formulating
- Strategic planning retreat
- Brainstorming
- Multivoting
- Prioritizing
- Reporting
- Synthesizing
- Value building

Conclusion

This book has been written as a call for change to all educators wherever they may be and whomever they may be—parents, professors, teachers, administrators, board officials, health and social service agency professionals, business executives, and community residents and taxpayers. We show how educators are awakening to the need to reconstitute our systems of learning for the well-being of all children, thereby once again bringing America to the forefront of the world economy, democracy, and technology.

America's education system is a case for action. As Peter Drucker wrote in the February 2, 1993, issue of the *Wall Street Journal*, "Whenever business keeps going downhill despite massive spending and heroic efforts by its people, the most likely cause is the obsolescence of its business theory."

The high-performance learning community is an outcome of organizational transformation that can occur in education as a result of systemic and systematic change. It guarantees the existence of the American public school system because it is learner centered, community based, and strategically managed. Most importantly, it meets the needs of current and future customers and is adaptable and flexible in a constantly changing, tumultuous environment.

Resources

The reinvention of education requires both systemic and systematic change. Chapter 2 addressed systemic change; here we present the rational, analytical, step-by-step, and collaborative processes of the systematic change.

Resource A, Systematic Planning Checklist, presents each of the attributes discussed in this book along with a checklist for action. Individuals interested in establishing high-performance learning communities may find this checklist helpful as they systematically plan and manage projects. However, the authors caution the reader regarding the use of procedures specified in the checklist. They serve only as guidelines for conducting systemic change and are not necessarily sequential, inclusive, nor foolproof. Moreover, nearly every procedure has accompanying tasks that are not included. Systemic change deals with integration of complex systems and processes and cannot be simplified to mere step-by-step applications. In addition, remember that inspired, energized, and visible leadership is critical to successful systemic change. In other words, the checklist is the "science" of the high-performance learning community, whereas leadership—expressed in acts of leadership and performance skills—is its "art."

Resource B, Competency Model for Curriculum Building, provides a more complete list of the acts of leadership and the performance skills—the critical factors for particular educational roles (see Chapter 3, Competencies). Instructional designers can use this model to develop effective training programs for individuals who want to create, lead, and manage the high-performance learning community.

Resource A
Systematic Planning Checklist

Key Attribute 1: World-Class Standards

- Conduct a benchmarking study.
- Identify learner competencies.
- Write standards for the identified competencies.
- Establish quality criteria for each standard.

Key Attribute 2: New Delivery System

- Design the teaching-learning system.
  - — Incorporate multiple methodologies.
  - — Use multiple media.
  - — Develop content-based, performance-based curriculum.
  - — Design a student progress assessment system.
- Clarify roles and expectations for teachers, team leaders, other educators, and the advisory board.
- Develop competency models of teachers, team leaders, and each of the other educational staff.
  - — Write position descriptions for the aforementioned persons.
  - — Design a competency-based performance management system.

Key Attribute 3: Integrated Services

- Identify the physical, intellectual, social, emotional, and spiritual needs of the learners for all developmental stages and ages.

- Assess the degree to which the current system meets those identified needs.
- Identify providers of community services to meet those identified needs that are not currently being met.
- Study each provider: (a) assess how the provider can help the educational system fulfill its mission, and (b) assess how the educational system can help the provider fulfill its mission.
- Establish a marketing strategy to promote the collaborative network comprised of those providers and the educational community.
- Meet with the decision maker of each provider to establish a collaborative network.
- Design a cross-training program so that educators and providers understand the basics of one another's functions.
- Develop an evaluation design to assess the effectiveness of the integrated delivery of services.

Key Attribute 4: Leading-Edge Technologies

- Write a technology plan to implement technology as an instructional, management, and communication tool to support the educational community.
- Base the plan on an educational analysis.
- Establish goals and objectives based on the outcomes of the analysis.
- Develop action plans.
- Design an evaluation process to assess the effectiveness of the technology plan.

Key Attribute 5: Shared Vision

- Write a personal vision statement.
- Establish the values or beliefs of the educational system with the stakeholders.
- Establish the purpose(s) of the educational system with the stakeholders.
- Develop the vision statement, i.e., the shared vision that reflects the values or beliefs and purpose.

- Identify obstacles to the realization of the shared vision.
- Develop an action plan to overcome or eliminate the obstacles.
- Refine one's personal vision statement in terms of the shared vision.

Key Attribute 6: Performance Management

- Design a student progress assessment subsystem that is appropriate for each student to measure his or her academic development for each significant learning episode.
- Develop a student-teaching team conferencing model.
- Design an accountability subsystem that addresses four measures—customer satisfaction, knowledge or skill acquisition, behavioral change, and organizational impact.
- Incorporate technology to manage the two subsystems.

Resource B
Competency Model for Curriculum Building

ACTS OF LEADERSHIP

1. Breaking paradigms
   - Being visionary (20+ years forward thinking)
   - Planning strategically
   - Planning operationally
   - Planning, implementing, managing, and evaluating change
   - Being open-minded
   - Having drive, energy, and courage
   - Establishing a climate that encourages responsible risk-taking

2. Establishing commitment
   - Building trust
   - Establishing rapport
   - Being congruent
   - Building a values-driven system
   - Establishing purpose

- Articulating support
- Aligning resources

3. Preparing for change

- Forming the leadership team
- Forming the action team(s)
- Evaluating the need for change
- Defining the future state
- Assessing the present state in terms of the future state
- Planning for the change
- Intervening at the individual level
- Intervening at the group level
- Intervening at the organizational level
- Managing the transition
- Monitoring the change
- Stabilizing the change
- Evaluating the change

4. Building collegiality

- Building group cohesion and teams
- Establishing mission, purpose, norms, and goals
- Clarifying expectations, roles, responsibilities, and relationships
- Contracting interpersonally
- Coaching
- Managing agreement
- Balancing tasks and attention to group members' needs
- Co-opting
- Identifying procedures and resources for accomplishing the work
- Respecting confidences
- Following up

5. Managing conflict

- Separating people from problems
- Focusing on interests, not positions
- Exploring interests
- Inventing options for mutual gain
- Developing multiple options for mutual gain
- Using objective criteria
- Getting commitment from each party on actions to solve the problem
- Following up

6. Planning strategically

- Using a wide variety of information as the basis for planning
- Eliciting appropriate participation from the staff and community to help develop and execute plans
- Scanning the internal environment
- Scanning the external environment
- Identifying values and beliefs
- Establishing mission and purposes
- Setting goals and objectives
- Ensuring that concrete, measurable, results-oriented, and achievable objectives are set and representative of all stated goals
- Assuring that resulting goals and objectives are based on well-defined and defensible needs
- Devising and implementing strategies and procedures to accomplish goals and objectives
- Developing action plans
- Aligning resources to execute the plans
- Monitoring the planning and implementation process
- Evaluating the plan
- Assuring that planning is a continuous process
- Establishing a rational procedure for developing and prioritizing goals and objectives
- Disseminating widely to constituents the resulting plan
- Generating support for the plan
- Seizing opportunities to reach goals and objectives

7. Making decisions

- Identifying and defining factors that inhibit or facilitate the progress of the organization
- Locating the causes of problems through data collection and analysis, using multiple methods and designs
- Using the talents and resources of the involved parties in making decisions
- Developing multiple tentative solutions with the involvement of others
- Modeling consensus building as a step toward constructive action
- Evaluating alternatives and their consequences
- Using creative approaches to making decisions

- Applying carefully conceived criteria to select the most viable course of action that will lead to the desired results
- Implementing effectively the chosen decision
- Establishing and maintaining the organizational structures necessary to executing the decisions
- Allocating effectively the resources to accomplishing the required tasks
- Supporting and sustaining decision-making efforts
- Monitoring progress and making necessary modifications
- Demonstrating flexibility when managing and using an appropriate style for the situation
- Evaluating the decisions
- Following up

PERFORMANCE SKILLS

1. Communicating skills (oral and written)
   - Nonverbal skills
     - Assessing and reacting appropriately to nonverbal clues
     - Demonstrating appropriate posture, gestures, and facial expressions
     - Listening to others
   - Verbal skills
     - Using positive phrasing
     - Using appropriate questioning skills
     - Using appropriate cognitive and affective responding skills
     - Using appropriate minimal encourages
     - Using appropriate paraphrasing skills
     - Using appropriate summarization skills
   - Giving convincing formal presentations and speeches using language and media appropriate to the target audience
   - Writing effective letters, reports, and other documents
   - Seeking and analyzing feedback to improve communication processes

2. Facilitating skills
   - Brainstorming
   - Building consensus

- Building teams
- Using process observation
- Assessing and analyzing group behaviors
- Building agendas
- Giving feedback
- Establishing collegiality
- Demonstrating collaborative team operations
- Conducting effective meetings

3. Gaining strength through diversity

- Assessing and analyzing cross-cultural value differences
- Assessing and analyzing intracultural value differences
- Assessing and analyzing socioeconomic value differences

4. Developing self

- Improving one's own professional skills and abilities through engaging in formal and informal professional growth experiences
- Participating in local, state, and national educational professional associations
- Participating in appropriate community, government, and political affairs
- Volunteering to do tasks that will help the organization and the community
- Writing an individual development plan
- Conducting educational research
- Reading voraciously educational literature and research results
- Considering one's own mistakes as opportunities for professional development
- Establishing a network of individuals with whom one can share new skills, receive coaching, and describe growth experiences

5. Developing staff

- Creating opportunities for staff growth as an essential means of developing and maintaining a healthy, effective organization
- Facilitating ongoing needs assessments to identify staff development areas that require attention
- Conferencing with staff and clarifying their professional goals; identifying areas for improvement; and aiding

them in coordinating individual objectives with those of the organization

- Involving staff in planning professional development experiences
- Giving staff members opportunities to use fully their current strengths and develop their potential abilities
- Using principles of learning, research findings, and change strategies when planning and providing staff development opportunities
- Arranging for staff to receive necessary education or training
- Providing mechanisms for staff to share new skills and describe growth experiences
- Establishing a climate where self-regulation and self-control provide the corrective force for improvement
- Coaching
- Giving observed praise and arranging for appropriate recognition
- Initiating personnel policies that reward staff who obtain and use knowledge and skills of value to the organization
- Writing an organizational long-range and short-range staff development plan
- Evaluating the staff development process and program

6. Marketing skills

- Developing a marketing plan
- Establishing rapport
- Identifying customer wants
- Describing product or service
- Matching product or service to customer wants; giving added value
- Persuading or influencing others
- Closing

Annotated Bibliography
and References

Annotated Bibliography

Adler, M. J. (1989). *Reforming education: The opening of the American mind*. New York: Macmillan.

Adler discusses his theories on education including interdisciplinary approaches, common curriculum, vocational education, and tracking. This book is a condensed version of his theories from previous work.

America 2000, plus a special section on national testing (1991, November). *Phi Delta Kappan*, pp. 185-251.

This issue contains four articles about the America 2000 national policy initiative and six about the concept of national testing as a reform strategy.

Berger, R. (1991). Building a school culture of high standards: A teacher's perspective. In V. Perrone (Ed.), *Expanding student assessment*. Association of Supervision and Curriculum Development.

Berger's interdisciplinary curriculum is based on the use and assessment of student projects. He stresses the importance of high quality, high standards, and high performance. He uses a variety of assessment methods in his classroom (tests, formal critiques, spontaneous critiques, student analysis of personal and peer work, and portfolios).

Bloom, B. S. (1981). *All our children learning.* New York: McGraw-Hill.

This is a summary of what we learned about education during the 1960s and 1970s. The book describes effects of research on our present understanding of the educational process, the relationships between the home and the school, the effects of instruction and curriculum on students, and the role of evaluation in determining the learning progress of individual students.

Boyer, E. L. (1983). *High school: A report on secondary education in America.* New York: Harper & Row.

In this report, Boyer addresses key issues concerning high school curriculum, organization, and instruction. He recommends the following for high schools: (1) Two thirds of the curriculum should be common core; (2) student tracking should be eliminated; (3) vocational education should be part of the electives; (4) electives should be limited to a planned cluster; (5) the school's organizational structure should be flexible; and (6) the principal should be the key educator.

Callahan, R. E. (1962). *Education and the cult of efficiency.* Chicago: University of Chicago Press.

This book traces the origin and development of the adoption of business values and practices in educational administration. The author contends that much of what has happened in American education can be explained on the basis of the extreme vulnerability of administrators to public criticism and pressure and that this vulnerability is built into our pattern of local support and control.

Carroll, J. B. (1963). A model of school learning. *Teachers College Record, 64,* 723-733.

Carroll has developed a school learning model that identifies key factors associated with achievement and attitudes of school children. Walberg and others have expanded the model to include the social environment of the classroom, the student's home environment, peer influences, and the effects of mass media.

Chittenden, E. (1991). Authentic assessment, evaluation, and documentation of student performance. In V. Perrone (Ed.), *Expanding student assessment*. Association for Supervision and Curriculum Development.

Chittenden presents a framework for assessment that includes observation of student performance, collection of performance samples, and testing (not necessarily standardized). According to Chittenden, alternative assessments should focus on classroom work, lead to greater and improved interaction between students and teachers, and serve as a source of information for accountability reports to students, parents and school districts.

Chubb, J. E., & Moe, T. M. (1990). *Politics, markets, and America's schools*. Washington, D.C.: The Brookings Institution.

This is a highly publicized study advocating a market approach to education. The authors build a case for allowing parents and students to have a "choice" of which schools the students attend.

Comer, J. P. (1990). Home, school, and academic learning. In J. I. Goodlad & P. Keating (Eds.), *Access to knowledge*. New York: College Board Publications.

Comer contends that all school personnel should work to establish bonds between students and teachers and between home and school. He maintains that each child must be socialized before he or she can be taught.

Cunningham, L. L. (1990). Reconstituting local government for well-being and education. In B. Mitchell & L. L. Cunningham (Eds.), *Educational leadership and changing contexts of families, communities, and schools: 89th Yearbook of the National Society for the Study of Education* (pp. 133-154). Chicago: University of Chicago Press.

Cunningham argues for systemic change in the structure of and management of local governments, including school districts. This involves the reconsideration of the philosophy, leadership, and management of local level instructions that affect the lives of children. He proposes a reconstituted local government focused on well-being and acknowledges education as primary to the quality of life for Americans of all ages.

Cunningham, L. L., & Children's Defense Fund. (1990). *Children 1990: A report card, briefing book, and action primer*. Washington, DC: Children's Defense Fund.

This publication provides information on the state of children's well-being in the United States. The report addresses issues related to children's health and nutrition, child care, and Head Start. It also provides statistics on key points.

Gagne, R. M. (1977). *The conditions of learning*. New York: Holt, Rinehart & Winston.

Gagne discusses what factors can really make a difference in instruction. This is described in two themes: varieties of learning outcomes and events of learning.

Glaser, R. (1977). *Adaptive education: Individual diversity and learning*. New York: Holt, Rinehart & Winston.

Glaser's book is a source of many principles for designing flexible, adaptable, learner-centered educational systems. He describes systems that could respond effectively to the various "needs, interests, abilities [competencies], talents, styles of learning, and styles of living" of individual learners. Glaser describes educational systems that have optional learning environments and multiple paths for each student.

Glaser, R. (1985). Learning and instruction: A letter for a time capsule. In S. F. Chipman, J. W. Segal, & R. Glaser (Eds.), *Thinking and learning skills* (Vol. 2). Hillsdale, NJ: Lawrence Erlbaum.

Glaser discusses the possibility of linking psychological theory and instruction practice in a systematic approach to fostering the acquisition of knowledge and skill. He also discusses the use of assessment and monitoring information for the effective guidance of learning.

Goodlad, J. I. (1984). *A place called school*. New York: McGraw-Hill.

An analysis of schools that has provided the basis for much of Goodlad's recent research and writing. The book identifies a number of the policies and practices that inhibit student success in school.

Haertel, G. D., Walberg, H. J., & Wang, M. C. (1990). What influences learning? A content analysis of review literature. *Journal of Educational Research, 84*(1), 30-43.

This is a careful analysis of the literature related to the factors that influence learning. The conclusions seem to indicate that single factors are not very important, but a combination of factors can make a significant difference in learning.

Johnson, R. T., & Johnson, D. W. (1990, January). Social skills for successful group work. *Educational Leadership*, 29-33.

The Johnsons contend that if the potential of cooperative learning is to be realized, students must be taught the prerequisite interpersonal and small-group skills and be motivated to use them. If teachers do so, they will not only increase student achievement, they will also increase students' future employability, career success, quality of relationships, and psychological health.

Kagan, S. L. (1991). Excellence in early childhood education: Defining characteristics and next-decade strategies. In S. L. Kagan (Ed.), *The care and education of America's young children: Obstacles and opportunities*. Chicago: University of Chicago Press.

Kagan suggests that we need a systemic, universal, and long-haul vision for early childhood education that balances private rights with public responsibility.

Kearns, D. T., & Doyal, D. P. (1988). *Winning the brain race: A bold plan to make our schools competitive*. San Francisco: Institute for Contemporary Studies.

This book emphasizes the importance of education from an economic point of view. Kearns and Doyal develop arguments to support a list of changes that would improve our current educational system.

Kirst, M. W., & McLaughlin, M. (1990). Rethinking policy for children: Implications for educational administration. In B. Mitchell & L. L. Cunningham (Eds.), *Educational leadership and changing contexts of families, communities, and schools*. Chicago: University of Chicago Press.

This chapter discusses the elements that shape children's experiences such as family income, parental employment, family structure, racial and ethnic background, health care, the availability of alcohol or other substances, and family support systems. The role of the school moves from being the "deliverer" of educational services to the role of broker of the multiple resources that can be applied to achieve successful, productive, and happy lives for children.

Kozol, J. (1991). *Savage inequalities*. New York: Crown/Random House.

Kozol describes what is happening to children from poor fami-
lies in the inner cities and the less affluent suburbs. He makes
a plea for fairness and decency in the way we pay for education
of all children in this country.

Maeroff, G. I. (1991, December). Assessing alternative assessment. *Phi Delta Kappan*, pp. 272-281.

In this article, Maeroff examined closely what is happening in
Rhode Island's pilot project for devising alternative assessment
methods. According to Maeroff, although alternative assess-
ment is attractive, its development and practice is "fraught
with complications and difficulties." He reported that "it is eas-
ier to propose outcomes than it is to set the criteria and establish
performance levels that are represented by various achieve-
ments."

Marshall, R. (1991). *Characteristics of high performance organizations.* Unpublished manuscript, University of Texas, Austin.

Some important outcomes of education are implied by the char-
acteristics described in Marshall's paper. According to Marshall,
high performance organizations need employees (managers and
workers) who work well in groups, who can use higher order
thinking skills, who are self-managers, who can perform a wide
variety of tasks, and who can effectively use leading-edge tech-
nologies.

Murphy, J., & Hallinger, P. (1986, May). The social context of effective schools. *American Journal of Education*, 329-355.

In this article, Murphy and Hallinger present results of a study
of effective schools. They examined the differences between
effective schools with high socioeconomic status and effective
schools with low socioeconomic status. They found that differ-
ences in socioeconomic status influenced differences in student
expectations, the frequency and nature of rewards, the role of
instructional leadership, and home-school cooperation.

Oakes, J., & Lipton, M. (1990). Tracking and ability grouping: A structural barrier to access and achievement. In J. I. Goodlad & P. Keating (Eds.), *Access to knowledge*. New York: College Board Publications.

Oakes and Lipton review the literature on tracking; consider
conventional arguments in its favor and responses that might

be made to those arguments; and scrutinize the early 20th-century beliefs, fears, and prejudices that helped spawn the practice.

Perrone, V. (1991). Introduction. In V. Perrone (Ed.), *Expanding student assessment.* Association for Supervision and Curriculum Development.

This book contains diverse chapters about alternatives to conventional assessment. It includes ideas for enriching assessment to overcome many of the problems of standardized testing, better support the decisions of teachers, and have a positive effect on teaching practices. Perrone is in favor of assessment practices "that are rooted principally in instructional programs, not apart from them, and that benefit students as they inform teachers."

Powell, A. B., Farrar, E., & Cohen, D. K. (1985). *The shopping mall high school: Winners and losers in the educational marketplace.* Boston: Houghton Mifflin.

This book has a good analysis of the history of the American high school. The implications of the philosophy and traditions that were established in the first 40 years of this century have had a lasting effect.

Sato, N., & McLaughlin, M. (1992, January). Context matters: Teaching in Japan and in the United States. *Phi Delta Kappan,* pp. 359-366.

This article reports findings from a comparative analysis of teaching in the U.S. and Japan. The data used in the study came from surveys of Japanese and U.S. teachers. The authors report that Japanese teachers work longer hours and more days than teachers in the U.S., are responsible for student behavior both on and off campus, have a greater degree of control of instructional matters, focus on "whole person" education, are more actively engaged in professional development activities, and participate in a broader range of school activities. Furthermore, Japanese schools are supported by a "mutually reinforcing network" of community institutions.

Schlechty, P. C. (1990). *Schools for the 21st Century.* San Francisco: Jossey-Bass.

This book addresses the educational needs of the learner in the 21st century. The discussion is focused on the types of jobs that will be needed and the types of changes that schools need to make to move away from the school "factory" model.

Sizer, T. R. (1984). *Horace's compromise: The dilemma of the American high school.* Boston: Houghton Mifflin.

This represents one of the major studies done on American high schools in the 1980s. The Coalition of Essential Schools was established as a direct result of the findings in this study.

Zessoules, R., & Gardner, H. (1991). Authentic assessment: Beyond the buzzword and into the classroom. In V. Perrone (Ed.), *Expanding student assessment.* Association of Supervision and Curriculum Development.

Zessoules and Gardner believe a skilled teacher assesses not only knowledge but also entire performances that are "sampled frequently over time in the classroom." They described an assessment "culture" that includes the following processes: (1) assessment being used as a vehicle for developing complex understandings; (2) students reflecting on their work and drawing new insights and ideas from it; (3) the evolution of student understanding being documented in the form of student "process-folios"; (4) and assessment being used as a means of provoking further learning.

REFERENCES

Adler, M. J. (1981). *Six great ideas*. New York: Macmillan.

American Association of School Administrators. (1988). *The educational administrator effectiveness profile*. Arlington, VA: AASA National Executive Development Center.

Coleman, P., & Larocque, L. (1988). *Reaching out: Instructional leadership in school districts*. Burnaby, British Columbia: Simon Fraser University and the Social Sciences and Humanities Research Council of Canada.

Comer, J. P. (1988). Educating poor minority children. *Scientific American, 259*(5), 42-48.

Cunningham, L. (1990). Reconstituting local government for well-being and education. In B. Mitchell & L. L. Cunningham (Eds.), *Educational leadership and changing contexts of families, communities, and schools: Eighty-ninth yearbook of the National Society for the Study of Education* (pp. 133-154). Chicago: University of Chicago Press.

Harris, B. M., & Wan, Y. (1991). *Performance criteria for school executives—Instructional Leadership Domain*. Austin: College of Education, University of Texas at Austin.

Marshall, R. (1991). *Characteristics of high performance organizations*. Unpublished manuscript, University of Texas, Austin.

Murphy, J., Hallinger, P., & Peterson, K. D. (1985). Supervising and evaluating principals: Lessons from effective districts. *Educational Leadership, 43*, 2.

Statistical Abstract of the United States, 1990. (1990). Washington, DC: U.S. Government Printing Office.

Toffler, A. (1991). *Power shift*. New York: Bantam Books.